Something Completely Odd

poems and ramblings

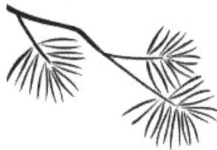

by Chris Dyer

Monday Creek Publishing
Ohio USA

Printed in the United States of America

Monday Creek Publishing, Ohio, USA
mondaycreekpublishing.com

I would like to dedicate this attempt at wordery to all, every creature human or otherwise. Walking in the street, sitting drinking tea, walking through a wood, a beach or the countryside, you are there...something that inspires me. Whether the inspiration be good or bad. To all the unsung heroes... not the rock stars. film stars, footballers (sorry a generalisation) that do things solely for their own publicity but the real people (and that includes some of the above) that I have met over the years that do things because they care because they have heart. The people that give a penny when they really cannot afford to. The people that offer friendship when they have no need to. The people that care.

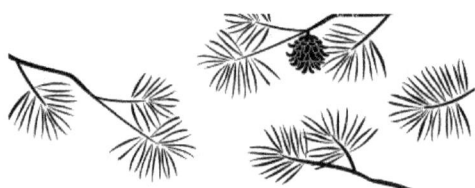

SUCH EYES

Such eyes, as deep as space,

A tender smile upon her face,

Hair so soft a pictures frame,

So, beautiful, a sweet refrain,

An angel found upon this Earth,

No gold or jewel can match her worth,

So when I sleep I'll think of her,

Then from my slumber never stir,

One breath of paradise upon my cheek,

I hope she finds the thing she seeks.

RETURN OF THE JESTER

Learn to laugh at yourself,

For the jester is not far,

If you can only laugh at others,

What mirth can you find?

If others are amused perhaps you can take from that?

Do not find offense find it in yourself to join the

amusements,

After all was it not you that was the jester?

HAVE YOU EVER...

Have you ever considered emotions, we are full of them after all! We laugh, cry, become depressed, get angry. The odd thing is that in the main the only emotion that is really worthwhile is laughter. Start laughing in a crowd and it is contagious, everyone around you becomes happy and their wellbeing level rises. Become angry and everyone surrounding us suffers just as much, sometimes more. I do not say that we can control our emotions all of the time but we can most of the time... odd? Think about a world leader that is in discussion with another world leader, we have all seen it... one becomes antagonised with the other and then the discussion falls into disarray... odd? Not really for if they had controlled their emotions then perhaps the war that was caused by a harmless comment such as... don't be an idiot becomes the start of thousands getting injured, maimed and killed... odd? True! If you or I did the same we would either be simply treated with contempt or taken to court and made to pay thousands for slander, politicians seem to be immune from this... odd! Very odd when you consider the possible ramifications! So, can we keep our emotions under control? Well we all 'lose the plot' on occasion... I did this morning and when I look back I must laugh because it was for no apparent reason and the only person that it affected in all honesty was me! Very odd! So, the next time you are about to allow your emotions try to find a little control before they race away with you… that would be odd but comfortingly sensible. Remember one thousand tears shed in joy are worthwhile one tear shed in sorrow is wasted.

AGAIN BECAUSE I LIKE IT!

No words to write from empty hearts,

No soul when souls are torn apart,

The millions that mattered not,

Yet no life thrives from empty pot,

To feel the void of pure despair,

To look not touch a fuse so fair,

From fiction life itself be born,

A curse, a talent, what was sworn?

Remember, words, remember me,

In years I may be then set free,

Why this ache so sharp so gay,

And yet alone so cold so grey,

The holding back, to test restraint,

My walls of black so bright you paint,

The lone wolf in his cloak of worldly sneers,

Pacing slowly through the years,

Pray don't look on him with such disdain,

Behind his eyes are tears of pain,

Yet look though through wooded hills he slinks,

Inside his heart like lamb he thinks.

THINK

Can we not see the things we miss,

As through our lives we plunder,

Unmoved, forgotten,

We tramp upon that which we tamed,

Unmoved by suffering and pain,

Complacent of all, arrogant,

What do you think as you read this?

Will you change... and think?

Will the hand that takes now give?

What do you think?

HOW HARD WAS THAT?

I see you and you see me,
Whatever will the outcome be?
I smile in hope and wait to see,
If maybe you smile back at me,
I take a step it's more in hope,
I swallow, it is hard to cope,
I say a word it is a jumble,
It sounds more like an insane mumble,
I know exactly what I want to say,
But there doesn't seem to be a way,
I am not asking you to bed,
And yet my face has still gone red,
A pretty lady standing there,
I swaggered up without a care,
Now I stammer like a fool,
And I really did think I was cool,
You look at me with half a smile,
Then stun me in your female guile,
Is there a hole, please swallow up,
This poor, poor man is just a pup.
And all of this as you will see,
To asked you. Join me for a tea?

TELLY

The advert shines upon the screen and off I go to shop,
I do not really want it but don't know how to stop,
The telly said it's useful a must for every home,
Now I ponder it in wonder as a king sits on his throne,
I don't know how to work it, I don't know what it's for,
It could be for the ceiling or maybe for the floor,
It doesn't play me music, it does not sweep or clean,
I'll watch again the advert upon the shiny screen,
It ends up in the cupboard with all the other "stuff",
I think I'll buy a vacuum to hoover up the dust,
The telly shows a new one I rush off to the shops,
Perhaps I'll sell the telly then at last perhaps I'll stop.

A PENCIL

In my hand I hold my world,

Is that what I become,

Without it I now feel naked,

Without it I feel lost and

The urgency to find a place to charge, save the data,

The fingers and thumbs frantically tapping at the
screen,

Breathless, yet I run nowhere, must get this message
sent,

Sent the wrong message to the wrong person,

Disaster!

Whatever happened to pen and paper?

MY LITTLE FRIEND

I am a little spider I am creeping up the wall,

I stick myself with cobweb to ensure that I don't fall,

I am not all that hairy but I scare you half to death,

Yet I run so fast from you that I cannot catch my breath,

I am just a little spider, I do not mean you harm,

If you let me I will tickle you as I crawl upon your arm,

So please I beg don't squish me, if you catch me with your eye,

The only thing I'm after is to rid you of your flies.

RAMBLING...

We do not think very much as humans! The one who has just jumped up red faced with rhetoric please read on before you utter more. Now this is odd...because we do think but we don't all at the same time! An example...lets rid ourselves of aphids...horrid little things eat all our vegetables! So our scientists think of a way to do it...odd...let's spray the little blighters with poison and rid the world of this awful pestilence...clever little scientists. Oh hang on a minute the spray we have used has also killed all the bees, no vegetables now as no pollination...odd and a big whoops! Now we have to go back a step and find what we call an alternative...actually it isn't because it has been there all along!

Odd...ladybirds, we all love ladybirds, cute little beetles with spots who would pass a plate of the most expensive caviar for one small munch on an aphid.... Haha...the simple answer our scientists come up with is we will breed ladybirds and they will eat the aphids...might not be quite as efficient as poisoning the local rivers, killing the bees and butterflies but at least we WILL have vegetables and vegetables that don't poison us as well because they have absorbed some of the toxins. I grew up mainly in the country-side and have spent most of my life in horses and farming. We now farm solely for profit, nothing wrong with profit, I like a profit as much as the next man, but now the farms are run by large conglomerates that know nothing of farming except how much the land will increase in value and how much profit they can squeeze from it. As a young man I can remember the "Old Fellows" rapturously telling me of the days they spent caring for their stock, note the word caring, we actually produce more food than we can ever use and yet a sizeable proportion of the world starves... economics? We can spend countless billions trying to nuke our neighbours or threaten them by building a bigger missile than them, does that signify something I wonder big missile big car... small minded politicians....

Think about that one, odd. We stuff everything full of hormones then wonder why it tastes all the same... we have complete disregard for the psychological effect on the other creatures as we push them into cages and environments that are totally alien and all for profit. Science is great but we forget that magic is science and science is magic by falling into the profit trap, remember though that magic comes from nature so where does science base itself? I once argued with someone that it was not only better to have a chicken that tasted and was reared traditionally than a chicken that didn't and was reared intensively, his reply was profit and of course how many more chicken he could rear than me...true? Odd...when he worked out how much he spent in electricity, high protein feeds, machinery, my profit margin whilst not as large as his was actually better percentage wise. My chickens lived a happy life, enjoyed scratching around and tasted so much better and in truth I felt much better, more relaxed and far less stressed than my friend. So should we try to consider not only profit but wellbeing, yes I think we should. Let the farmers farm and the conglomerates conglomerate. Nature will never be subdued or die regardless of what we do, it will always be there, we are the ones that need to worry. It is extremely easy to make a point, man controls the planet, actually we don't, we might think we do but nah! Get rid of a tiny little creature the bee, and the world starts to die, that must tell you something. A wise old farmer once said to me that everything nature gives us has a purpose, it might not be immediately obvious but as sure as eggs are eggs it will have a purpose…he finished by saying remember my son nothing nature produces is worthless.

Now I finish this rambling with another point. Throughout the ages we have, as can be proved by Stone age paintings, believed in deities. It doesn't matter what you wish to call your God but if you are one of the majority that believes there is a supernatural entity, surely it is one and the same? Why then do we kill and maim each other for the sake of a name? I am no expert, but I am pretty certain that someone someday is going to get an awfully big shock when it is pointed out to them personally! Before you take another bite out of your king-size extra super-duper whopper-mega burger, think of how many hungry children you will feed with what you throw away, and how much better it would be if the burger you bit into tasted a little more like beef that had at least had some form or a natural life and a little less like a chemical concoction. I am having a steak for dinner and I am proud to say it is from an outdoor reared cow that has tasted grass and had a life. We are omnivores, we can't any more than a lion, eat solely Brussel sprouts (and I do like Brussel sprouts and yes I know I have said very similar before) but we do not have the absolute right to misuse the intellect and power given to us. Can't stop once I have started! I would like to encourage everyone to check out PASA on the dreaded internet…they do a great job trying to save our cousins, so take a look.

Think of this as well, there are what about 7 billion humans? Odd. No mammoths, no dodo's, around 14,000 lions (used as a symbol all over the world), most of which are in captivity, just over 600 Ethiopian wolves, a few thousand rhino and tiger. Let us not hang our heads in shame when the children of the future ask to see one of these magnificent creatures and we have to tell them just like the mammoth and the dodo, we drove them to extinction. Oh, and I can tell you truthfully, I stroked a rhino and it is not only humbling but a great privilege.

If I can change, you can change and if you can change, the politicians can change and the world can change and then we all benefit.

Wow I do go on a bit!

BLACKTHORN WOODS

The sound came and went, causing the boys to start. The silence was almost as frightening as the noise, waiting for the next rustle, the next dry twig to crack. "I knew it was a mistake to come, we're going to end up being eaten or something!" The heaviest set of the three boys said, his teeth chattered though it was a warm balmy night.

A skinny boy with round spectacles who sat in the corner of the tent with a metal mug of steaming soup looked up and smiled. "It was you that said we should do it Billy. Let's camp out in Blackthorn Wood you said…it's a Full Moon tonight you said…we'll capture the monster you said…we'll be heroes you said!"

"Shut up, four eyes! I know what I said, but I didn't think we'd end up getting eaten!"

"You're scared!"

"I'll show you scared Steve Thomas you scrawny worm!" The bigger boy made to move towards him but just as he did there was a loud growl just outside the tent and he froze. "I wanna go home!" he almost cried, and he slumped shaking in the far corner of the tent and started sobbing.

"It's just the wind," Steve scoffed, "you coming John? I'm going to take a look."

"No way… I'm not going out there to get eaten! *T..t that's the monster!*" he stammered.

Though Steve was very near as afraid as his friends, he was not going to show them and scrambled his way out of the tent into the dark foreboding woods. He had spent too many nights sitting alone in an orphanage and this adventure was respite from his normal life. He could not go back anyway, his friends would go back to the welcoming arms of a mother. He would go back to a stern telling off or worse, there would be no welcoming arms for him. Shining his torch around the small clearing where they had pitched their tent, he swung the beam slowly on the dense undergrowth he very nearly wet himself. Standing right at the edge of the trees was a figure. He gulped and though shaking, moved forward.

For years the Blackthorn Wood monster has been the talk of the village, some laughed and said it was all a joke but most, in fact even those that called it a joke, avoided the woods after dark. When Billy had announced to "his gang", namely John his cousin and Steve his neighbor, but one and the only other boy of the same age in the village, that they were going to trap the monster, the other "gang members" agreed, in truth, they had not expected it would ever come to fruition.

"Who is it?" he stuttered but there was no response, the figure just stood there unmoving, bright green eyes staring at him. He took another step forward, now almost close enough to touch the figure. "I know you boy!" the voice was deep and guttural and made Steve start. "Even though you fear you still come forward... come follow me I will not harm you." Steve was now close enough to see the figure in more detail. The face was covered with hair and as he spoke Steve could almost see his reflection in the whiteness of its teeth. "Come boy," the figure almost growled. And Steve followed, his curiosity overcoming his fear. It seemed like hours as he stumbled along behind the figure, but in truth it was but a few minutes, maybe ten, maybe fifteen, before the figure stopped and raised his head towards the sky and let forth a howl. Steve let out an involuntary gasp and the figure turned towards him. "Do not be afraid little pup, stand still and let my family introduce themselves." Steve looked around nervously as dark shapes silently appeared from the undergrowth. He could not help himself, his teeth chattered in fear.

Locals stayed well clear of Blackthorn Woods. As far back as anyone could remember not one person had gone further than a few yards into the foreboding trees. Not for a long, long time. It started when the old Blacksmith had been cutting down a large Ash tree to feed his forge and had spotted a wolf watching him from the undergrowth, he threw his axe at the creature but before it made contact something jumped from the undergrowth and caught it. He ran and the tale he told became more and more exaggerated as time passed. No one dis-believed him, for his hair turned white even before he had ran hell for leather from the woods. Before long the tale had reached epic proportions and to enter the woods was certain death. The blacksmith was a lucky man to have escaped with his life. Why if he had not the strength of five men the creature would have had him, as it was he managed to fight his way back with only a few scrapes and bruises (actually, caused by his panicked run through the undergrowth but now attributed to his valiant fight with the creature). As long as the villagers stayed within a few yards of the woods, no harm befell them. A few puffed out their chests and ventured further but always came back shaking their hair white and tales of a monstrous creature that had chased them teeth bared and ready for blood. Everyone now steered clear of the woods. No one ever considered why they had no need to venture into the woods themselves though, there always seemed to be plenty of deadwood a few feet in the trees, there was always lots of fruits and nuts scattered on the leafy carpet. Though nobody ever questioned why as there were not enough fruit and nut trees to produce such a bounty, they just took it for granted and kept their fear of entering the woods proper.

Slowly the shapes came closer to Steve, carefully coming up to him sniffing, his legs, his hands. "Meet my family, are they not beautiful?" The figure almost growled. "They like you...good." Steve was still frightened but his curiosity had been ignited. Tentatively he reached down as what was obviously a very young jet black wolf approached him with what seemed almost as much fear as he felt himself. His hand touched the wolf's ear and Steve noticed how soft it felt beneath his fingers. The wolf looked at him, her yellow eyes staring for a moment then pushed her nose onto Steve's hand and gently licked his fingers. In that instant, all of Steve's fear disappeared and he knelt in front of the wolf stroking its neck with both hands. The wolf responded by leaning into Steve. "Come pup, now you see there is no harm here. My family is not your enemy, we only ever kill to eat or to defend ourselves… we are not like the human race… we do not kill for fun." Steve had not realised that the time had passed and the first glint of the sun was rising slowly from its slumber. He could now see the figure clearly and realised it was not some monster but a man, he looked almost as much wolf as man but he was, there was no doubt, a man. "I have a favour I would ask of you and in return I shall give you a gift that no other can for I am the last of my kind." Steve made to speak, but the man held up his hand to silence him. "I am a mage, a wizard, a sorcerer, whatever name man wishes to give me. I have watched these woods and my children for many years. It is also the last of its kind. Man has destroyed all else taking the magic for profit and leaving behind nothing. Old trees full of the wonder of nature are felled and a tree planted that grows for the blink of my eye, then it is felled itself for profit and greed, the Earth has no time to give it the magic it processes. Slowly we kill all around us except here. Blackthorn Wood as you call it is the last place, if it is not kept and nurtured then the land will shrivel. I am tired and old, I have no wish to harm, my children only wish to live, but man will not let them, they desire all that they see and it does not matter if in taking it they destroy themselves. I am here to protect both my children and mankind itself. If I give you a gift will you tell a tale for me?" Steve found himself nodding he felt so at peace, almost hypnotised.

"I will warn you, it will be uncomfortable but I can promise you in time you will know how great a gift it will be." Again Steve nodded. "Be strong then young pup." Then with a small gesture of his hand Steve watched as the wolves started towards him. He felt their teeth as they sunk into his arm, not deep but still painful, then another set on his leg, then another, tears welled in his eyes and he sunk to the ground as more teeth punctured his skin and he sank into darkness. When he awoke it was dark and he did not realise at first he could see as clear as if it were day and yet his glasses were gone. He looked around and though unsure thought he must be lying in the trunk of some enormous tree, beneath him was not cold earth but soft moss. He looked around automatically for his glasses before realizing again that he could see perfectly well. If this was a tree, it had to be bigger than anything he could have imagined, it seemed to be bigger than the village hall. Sitting at a table in the centre was the mage. He was smiling. "Ah you are awake pup... how do you feel? Are you hungry?"

"What... Why...?"

The mage laughed and it was like bells ringing joyfully on a bright clear morning. "Eat first pup, there is plenty of time for questions... and of course answers!"

A beautiful girl with long black hair and yellow eyes came from somewhere in the shadows carrying a tray of steaming food. When Steve looked at her his stomach filled with butterflies. There was something strangely familiar about her. She smiled at Steve and his heart beat faster. "You chose well Faylin, he will make a good and true mate." Faylin lowered her eyes demurely.

"Now eat pup and I shall answer your questions... there is no need to ask for I already know what they are," he said smiling. "When each of my family nipped you, each gave a little of themselves, each gave you a little magic, a little strength. I am sure you see...," he laughed again... "that you have no need for glasses... in fact I am sure you must be surprised at how good you can see, probably better than all others, you are now shall we say... different, you will see better, hear better, smell better than any other and most of all you will think better."

Steve woke and looked over at Faylin who was curled up, in fifty years she was still as beautiful as the first time he had seen her. His notoriety as the boy that had escaped the wolf pack was long forgotten, his career as a politician outstanding, he had changed the world literally and if only his voters knew more than likely saved it. He had with his electoral power put a protection order on Blackthorn Wood, some had not liked it but then few had any taste to argue with Steve, there is something wolfish about that man one of his opponents had said. Blackthorn Wood was kept safe and free from interference. Some said Steve had protected it because there was some sort of secret government base hidden deep in the trees, some just thought Steve was a bit odd but feared to question his motives when the electrified fence was put in place. Faylin and Steve knew different, they would often enter the woods in the dead of night and meet with their family, run and take pleasure in the hunt and the closeness of family. Tonight, would be different though, it was Mike that would run with them, Mike who would meet the mage and Mike who would be given the gift. Mike entered the bedroom. His tousled hair unruly as ever, his thick glasses perched on the end of his nose. "Mum, do we have to go camping tonight? Can't you talk Dad out of it? He always listens to you."

"No dear, tonight we go camping just like your Dad says. Tonight we will be a family."

ODD

Love is the strangest of emotion,

It reaches inside of you and lifts you to the Heavens,

It holds you there floating in its airy paradise,

Then suddenly dashes you to the ground holding out its hand to save you just before you break,

It holds your heart and squeezes, a pain like no other,

Then relaxes its grip and allows you to feel the euphoria once again,

A fairground ride, a rollercoaster, we desire it yet abhor it,

We seek it yet run from it,

We have yet to find a way to hide from it.

DEFINITE

A valentine I think of,

Anonymous, too shy,

A card that speaks of unrequited love,

An unknown universe, an empty space,

A heart so true and yet unfamed,

Afraid to utter words, afraid to move,

Valentine lost in love yet so did his object,

Both afraid to say, both with eyes cast down,

One word was all it takes and hearts flutter or break,

No term of time to suffer,

Better to face the truth than hide behind it,

A card yes and a word? Definitely.

JUST ONE THING

One sweet kiss is all I wish,

A tender touch upon my wrist,

The warmth, the feel one sweet embrace,

Just that moment my pulse to race,

One smile one hand is all I need,

My heart has only care not greed,

I wish for all the same as me,

To soar in perfect ecstasy,

For eyes of truth to look, to see,

That this one thing will set us free.

ONE MORE

One more before I rest my head,

And slumber restlessly in bed,

One more thought, one small delay,

Before I end another day,

No tear but sorrow lies,

I find it hard to still my eyes,

I search my heart and wonder find,

For lies to treat my soul unkind,

Even then the protests rise,

It was not true it's my demise,

Now upon the pillow rest my head,

I need to dream my ego fed,

Then wake with hope and even joy,

A plan of sense I must employ,

You are no different to me,

We are all blind and do not see.

A PENGUIN

I would like to be a penguin,

Sliding on the ice,

I think to be a penguin would be rather nice,

I would not sing, but make a croak,

And when I swim would not get soaked,

I'd be so fast the polar bear,

Would never catch me in his lair,

But wait, although I'm rather cute,

That human stick at me might shoot,

Then wow this ice is awfully cold,

And penguins eat raw fish I'm told,

So just perhaps I'd better stay,

A human for another day!

ANGER

Anger just a scream and shout,

Tell me what's that all about?

Make a judgement, make it bad,

Just because you're feeling mad,

Easy though to say calm down,

When all that you can do is frown,

Take a walk or take a breath,

Before it worries you to death.

TODAY

Today should be a good day,

The sky is blue, the sun shines,

Yet it rains, and my soul is black,

Today should be a good day,

I have good health,

Yet I am in pain,

Today should be a good day,

I see, I hear, I taste,

Yet my heart is heavy,

Today should be a good day,

I have friends, I have joy,

Yet still I have sadness.

BERT

I have a little beetle,

I think I'll call him Bert,

I'll house him in a matchbox,

He's just a little squirt,

He isn't very clever,

He bashes into things,

Though I tried to teach him jumping through a ring,

I think that Bert needs freedom,

And so I'll let him go,

Then maybe in the wilderness Bertie boy will grow.

DINGLY DELL

My laptop is evolving,
But can it make the tea?
It tried to boil the kettle,
But it would not work for me,
I told it how to do it,
But it didn't even try,
It really is enough to make a person cry,
Now it can send a letter,
And do all sorts of stuff,
But can it make a sandwich or hoover up the fluff?
No, it's still a laptop that I cannot be without,
But it cannot cook my dinner or peel a Brussel sprout,
I wonder what it thinks of me if it waits for me to start?
I wonder if it dreams when the plug is out at dark?

SMUG

Easy as you stand there a smug look on your face,

A hypocrite, a contradiction,

How many people will the concrete feed?

How many children or species will it save?

You wave your arms in bluster as you wish to build a wall,

How can a man tell you that when he cannot look to himself?

Build a wall and stop them when his hand holds?

When you are one yourself how can you despise another?

Will it make a difference or fuel more hatred?

Look what hatred has done in history,

Still we have not learned,

Walls will not stop them, it is a lie to fool us all,

Stand as one people, colour, creed or religion does not matter,

We built the Berlin Wall and knocked it down,

Barriers do not work,

We must stand strong, together as one people,

Not alienate ourselves from others or they will turn a blind eye to you,

Ours are no different than yours, self-gratification,

Pander to the whims of the one that shouts,
They are the ones that want this for they are the
ones that do not care.

DREAM

How we dream and reach,

To grasp that moment as intangible as smoke,

To wake and think a thought is real,

To yearn to return, our thoughts so vivid,

To walk the endless day waiting for the night,

To lie and wait for sleep in hope,

How we wish to dream.

FIVE LEAVES

She stands tall,

Her dress no longer green,

Falling from her slender body,

Hues of red and gold,

Shimmering in the watery sun as it falls,

Still beautiful as she lays a soft bed upon the floor,

Giving her life blood to rejuvenate,

She will soon stand naked her five leaves left.

QUICKSAND

Step onto the quicksand,

No branch to hold,

No saviour here to grasp your wrist,

Slowly you sink, your breath becomes short,

Vision fades as you are squeezed,

You struggle vainly, fight,

But you cannot win,

Sinking is inevitable,

As darkness encompasses you,

You will see the smile that took you there.

CLIMB

I can smile and climb a tree,

I see you do you see me?

We are alike but still not friends,

Yet have a past that cannot end,

I could be you, a twist of fate,

And yet from me you still must take,

I walk the ground not quite like you,

But we are cousins that is true,

You treat me poor for your own gain,

Show no respect, that is quite plain,

But I can smile and climb a tree,

So, tell me now what could I be?

WHAT?

I am wider than I am long,

Yet longer than I am wide,

I am only worth when I am bent,

And lucky when hung,

I am walked upon,

I am raced,

You can hear me,

I am fitted yet can be lost,

What am I?

START

Of all we do of all we see,

What do you think when you see me?

Do you wonder? Do you care?

If she has brown or golden hair,

Do you say the things you think,

Or hide your eyes as past you slink,

One word hello would be a start,

And then another before you part,

That one small move may lift esteem,

Then maybe you will find your dream.

MATILDA

At the bottom of our garden,

Matilda has a pen,

Matilda's not a chicken,

Matilda is a hen,

She might lay eggs I think she could,

I made a comfy nest of wood,

And every day I go and look,

In every crevice, every nook,

But no, my hopes must take a knock,

Matilda turned out as a cock.

WHAT?

What would I be?

If I was not me?

An astronaut, a star,

Drive a faster car,

Then pay the fines for speeding,

Something I'm not needing,

The mirror calls so take a look,

And see the cover of the book,

Write the words with zest,

And then see that you are best.

PROVIDER

I have two wings and I can fly,

Though scientist still wonder why,

You wave your arms when I'm around,

Try to knock me to the ground,

I make you something you desire,

Full of health and life's own fire,

I never stop I always work,

And in my duty never shirk,

I even pollinate for you,

It's so important what I do,

So please don't bash me to the ground,

And do not wave your arms around,

I do not sting if you leave me,

I am a simple bumble bee.

THE DOOR

Be shocked when you see,

What happens when the door is closed,

The one that made you laugh,

Now makes another cry,

No smile now through the gritted teeth,

No joke no laughter,

I wonder what you will see,

When the door closes.

WHAT A DRAG

I've given up the dreaded fag,

Though still would love to have a drag,

Electronic is what I now puff,

Though giving up is still so tough,

In truth, upon another suck,

Though hope to give it up with luck,

It's now the vapour that I crave,

And without it, start to rave,

I wonder if I might succeed,

To bin this thing I do not need.

BLUE

When I am sad and feeling blue,

It's not just me it's also you,

If I am happy then you smile,

It's better by a hundred miles.

JELLY

If I was a jelly I would shiver with delight,
You may think I'm a scaredy cat and shiver just with
fright,
I am the best at parties because I am such fun,
I'm fruity as you chase me around the plate I run,
And now I am a trifle with custard and with cream,
A shivering little jelly that makes a childhood dream.

Ramble...

Get ready it's another ramble! I would like to promote something to all men. It isn't something that I want to sell, it isn't anything that will cost you, but it is something that will stand you proud. My father often said to me that the only thing in life that was totally free is good manners. If you think about it there may be other things but manners don't cost you anything at all. I lived in Africa for a long time and whilst I have quite a few friends there was always amazed at the difference in culture and the reaction to a different culture. I used to say thank you and please as example when being served in a shop. Most shop assistants were stunned, very appreciative but stunned because it was believed unnecessary as they were being paid to serve you. I had some really strange responses, yet all of them not only surprised but appreciative. Perhaps we can all learn something from that. I am now back in the UK and am pleased to say that I have found that for the most part manners are still an integral part of the culture. What amazes me is even if saying please and thank you, opening a door for a lady (for the macho men, it isn't wussie, for the feminist it isn't an insult) is still for the most part welcomed. So guys, it doesn't matter if you have arms like superman, or wear a leather, have cropped hair or are covered in tattoos, be a gentleman, show the world it is not the cover but the contents that make the book, and manners maketh man. Oh and when you go home from work today and walk in the house, try something, tell your wife or your girlfriend (boyfriend not to offend the ladies) that you think they look wonderful, maybe even take the bull by the horns and tell them they are the most important thing to you and that you love them. I promise you the difference in that small gesture will turn your world into a sunny day. If it doesn't work then you can always email me and give me an ear bashing... don't think my ears have anything to be worried about though!

WELLY BOOTS

Wellies green and wellies black,
For squelching up that muddy track,
Now wellies come in many hues,
There's yellow, red and even blue,
To keep you dry when there's a flood,
Wellies made to walk in mud!

WHEN

When the blood dries,

Will you hear the cries,

The children lost the mothers grief,

The paper signed was yet so brief,

Now look around and what is left,

One signature and all bereft,

So now you laugh and take a bow,

But take another look at now,

You made a promise, a better life,

But all you've managed is more strife,

The button red you wait to press,

You tell them it will end the mess,

But think of this when all alone,

No place that we can call a home,

Pray to your God perhaps you'll see,

The suffering you cause for me.

When will you learn, when life is gone?

Too late to see you got it wrong.

SWALLOW

I watched a swallow flit and dive,

The master of the pale blue skies,

A fighter pilot of the air,

Catching bugs without a care,

An air display none can compare,

A fighter pilot of the air.

GESTURE

One small thing is all you need,

Just once a day, one good deed,

Give a penny give a smile,

Give a yard or give a mile,

One small gesture, what a gift,

Instead of conflict heal the rift.

WRITE

What do I get from reading,

A movie played before my eyes,

Pictures played inside my head,

Yet no screen I need,

Just small black squiggles based on white,

It is for you the things I write.

IF I WAS

If I was an octopus,

With suckers on my arms,

I wrap you in my embrace and ink you with my charm,

If I was a cheetah,

I chase right after you,

I'd trip you with my dew claw and knock you all askew,

if I was an eagle,

My wings so strong and wide,

I'd grab you with my talons and in the clouds we'd glide,

It's all romantic nonsense and it's never going to be,

I think I'll give up writing and make a cup of tea.

You probably think I am some sort of hippy...I am definitely not, I have a history just as I am sure if you are honest you do, but I am still just an ordinary guy, just average...a little opinionated perhaps and probably as much a hypocrite as anyone. I do things wrongly just as you, I try to be honest and for the most part succeed. I have all the emotions that we all have, though am probably a little too outspoken for most people's tastes. I have a temper, which I try hard to curb and I have a voice which I try to use but control! If you read my words I hope that just maybe in one or two of them you may find something in common, something that makes you wonder or smile. You know we seem to forget, rich or poor, good or bad we all travel towards the same place.

Thanks for taking the time to read this and I hope it made you smile in places and think in others, most important I hope you found some pleasure in it.

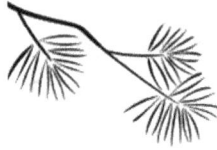

Something Completely Odd
poems and ramblings

Chris Dyer
www.chrisdyerauthor.com

About the Author

Although I have always enjoyed writing my love for horses has been instrumental in most of my books, and my knowledge, which I class myself fortunate to have gathered, as it has helped me in my writing. It has also given me the opportunity to formulate natural remedies for horses. I have an association with an international equine products company. Who are very demanding in their requirements, of which I am glad, and I have produced several formulas that I hope they will market once trials are completed. I would say to all that I feel blessed as I am doing the things that I love to do. It is hard work and I have to say it hasn't always been like this… like everyone, there have been serious low points in my life, even to the point of living on a beach wondering where my next meal would come from. I hope as you read this you will have determination and "never say die". Whatever you are doing or wish to do keep at it, there is a strong possibility that if you are determined enough it will come through for you in the end.

Titles from Chris Dyer

The Beginning: Book One The Sapphire Staff
Plants Potions and Oils For Horses, J.A. Allen (Crowood Press)

The Rocket Series:
Sting in the Tail
From Rocket with Love
Storm Brewing
(Monday Creek Publishing 2017)

Something Completely Different: Poems, Proverbs, Rhymes
Something Completely Weird: Poems, Proverbs and Stuff
Something Completely Odd: Poems and Ramblings
Something Completely Crazy: More Poems and Ramblings
(Monday Creek Publishing 2017)

www.ingramcontent.com/pod-product-compliance
Lightning Source LLC
Chambersburg PA
CBHW071429040426
42445CB00012BA/1310